Y0-BDK-070

Studies In
Christian Stewardship

BY

C. J. SHARP

Author of: "New Training for Service," "The Church of the New Testament," "New Testament Evangelism," "Personal Evangelism," "The Christ of the Four Gospels."

THE STANDARD PUBLISHING COMPANY
CINCINNATI, OHIO

Copyright, 1954
THE STANDARD PUBLISHING COMPANY
Cincinnati, Ohio

Printed in U. S. A.

CONTENTS

(CONTENTS CONCLUDED)

FOREWORD

There is both a need and a constant demand for a study on Christian stewardship that is an advance in New Testament knowledge on the subject. There have been produced many books and tracts on the subject, some as definite presentations to promote tithing, some appearing to have back of them no higher motive than to serve as a means to call forth more cash for some agency, enterprise, or cause.

We have noted that practically all of these presentations rely on arguments to show that stewardship is an obligatory duty, based on the law. In other words, the arguments set forth the claim that tithing is an established principle of the Mosaic law or of the pre-Mosaic law, which is claimed not to have been abrogated when the Mosaic law was superseded by the gospel of Christ.

In these lessons we shall attempt to present the reasons for Christian stewardship from the teachings of Christ and the New Testament under which we now live in this, the Christian or gospel dispensation. We may and do make use of established facts or truths found in the Old Testament, that are unquestioned by any and all Christians. An example would be: that *God is the creator of all*. But the basis for Christian stewardship must be found in and based on the teachings of Christ and the apostles, as found in the New Testament, and on the basis that it contains all the needed instruction for Christian life, practice, and procedure, and is sufficient in itself to that end.

BASIC FACTS, TRUTHS, AND PRINCIPLES TO BE RECOGNIZED AND FOLLOWED

Anything That Is To Stand or Be Relied Upon Must Rest on a Solid, Unshakable Base

Anything, whether physical, mental, or spiritual, must have a solid, unquestioned, and sure foundation to rest upon if it is to stand and endure. This applies in the material, mental, and spiritual realms. It applies to our attitudes and relations to God and to our wholehearted faith in Him, as well as to our acts in relation to Him. By foundations we mean established facts, established truths, and established principles.

What facts are, what truth is, and what are principles, can be determined in four ways:

1. *Self - evident Truths.* While mathematics is termed an *exact science,* and depends on accurate and conclusive proof and demonstration of proved logical conclusions, yet *all* mathematics start with, and rest on, certain truths which no one can prove, but which no one questions. For example: "Things equal to the same thing are equal to each other." It's evidence is in itself. In logical reasoning, we may cite, "That which is designed has to have a designer" or "That which is created has to have a creator." These are called "self-evident truths."

2. *Demonstrated Truths.* Demonstrated truths are those proved by research, experimentation, and

tests multiplied to unquestioned conclusion. Science depends on this kind of facts and truths, and when proved to be universal they are usually termed *laws of nature*. As an example would be, "Every particle of matter in the universe attracts every other particle with a force varying directly as the product of the mass and inversely as the cube of the distance between the centers of mass." These truths may be called *discovered* truths about the universe, left by the Creator to be revealed through man's intelligence and enterprise. Truths concerning the atom would serve as an illustration.

3. *Historical Facts and Truths.* Historical facts are based on personal knowledge of events definitely known and recorded. There is thus a world full of historical facts, established and unquestioned. These truths might be illustrated by the fact that Nero was emperor of Rome, or that Grant was a general of the Union Army.

4. *Revealed Facts and Truths.* There is a certain class of both facts and truths which man alone is incapable of discovering by any degree of research or reasoning. Only an all-wise and merciful God, Creator of heaven and earth, could know or make these known. When made known to man by the Creator these truths are known as *"revealed truths."* We find these truths solely in the Bible; for example: "God created man in his own image," or "God created the heaven and the earth," and "The wages of sin is death; but the gift of God is eternal life through Jesus Christ our Lord." In these revealed truths we

[8]

would include such direct commands and instructions contained in the New Testament, such as "Repent, and be baptized . . . for the remission of sins," and "Go ye therefore, and teach all nations, baptizing them in the name of the Father, and of the Son, and of the Holy Ghost." We should also include such general practices of early New Testament Christians as were sanctioned by the divinely inspired apostles.

Every conclusion as to our relationship and obligations must be based on one of these fundamental truths or principles.

A Distinction Between Truths and Facts

Truths and facts are sometimes identical but not always so. A *truth* is eternal, unwavering, and unchangeable. Facts may be but temporary, but not necessarily so. For example, it is a fact that Dwight Eisenhower is the President of the United States, but in time it will not be so. It is a fact that George Washington was the first President of the United States and that fact will remain.

A *truth*, once discovered or revealed, remains so long as the world shall stand. A principle is defined as "A fundamental truth; a settled rule of action; a fixed governing law of belief or action, which exercises a directing influence in life, action, and behavior." An example would be the principle determining every act of Jesus. This principle was an absolute trust in the heavenly Father, and loyalty and unquestioning submission to Him in all things. This principle was certainly based on His unerring and complete knowledge of the truth about God.

The Earth Is God's, Not Ours

We may assent to the fact that the earth is God's, and recognize it as a fact or truth and yet not acknowledge it in our lives and practice. This is one of the revealed truths (Deuteronomy 10: 14). Any argument or proof offered in this study as to the part and place of Christian stewardship in the Christian's life is to be brought from the teachings of Christ and the apostles as found in the New Testament, and in no sense is based on the law of the Old Testament, either Mosaic or pre-Mosaic. Yet we deem it wise to include some of the facts and truths stated clearly in the Old Testament that are unquestioned by Christians, and principles that have obtained since creation. Here we must recall that distinction is to be made among laws established by fiat, facts established by history, and truths that obtain eternally.

The first face to recognize is: "The earth is the Lord's and the fulness thereof; the world, and they that dwell therein" (Psalm 24: 1). This is a statement of David, to which many other statements may be added (See Deuteronomy 10: 14; 1 Kings 20: 3; Ezekiel 18: 3, 4; Genesis 1: 1). These are statements of fact, not laws of procedure. They are *revealed* facts and truths.

Until one recognizes this first great truth, and accepts it with both head and heart, it is with little profit or understanding that he should attempt to understand and apply the teachings of Christ and the New Testament in application to Christian life.

Our Tenure of the Earth Is Temporary

The second fact to be recognized is that our tenure of a minute portion of the earth is but temporary. This fact does not even need a Scriptural statement. It is one of the sure things demonstrated by universal experience since time began. Some one has put it, "there are no pockets in shrouds." What I do with the money or possessions that pass through my hands, and which I think I *own*, will be done here and now. The same is true of my talents, my abilities, my time, and my influence for good and for God. "Now is the day of salvation" (2 Corinthians 6: 2).

An overemphasis can be placed on money alone. In many ways it is the least important item that one can render to God. A life committed and consecrated to Him may and can be of greater service than a million dollars. A life so committed will also solve the stewardship matter automatically.

Not Only What I Have, But I Myself Am God's

It is a further fact that, as a Christian, I am God's and Christ's. When I became a Christian, I not only made Christ mine but it is also true that at the same time I became His. When I was baptized into Christ I became a new creature in Christ. My hope and my only hope and promise for eternal life in heaven rests not on my good morals but that *I am His.* In Revelation it is stated, Blessed are they that do his commandments, that they have right to the tree of life, and enter in through the gates into the city" (Revelation 22: 14), or "No man cometh unto the Father but by me" (John 14: 6), or, as Paul said, "Ye are Christ's; and Christ is God's" (1 Corinthians 3: 23), or again, "There is therefore now no condemnation to them that are in Christ Jesus, who walk not after the flesh, but after the Spirit" (Romans 8: 1).

Recognizing this fact means that I am to serve Him with all that I have and all that I am. I have, as a Christian, accepted Him not only as Saviour, but as my Lord and Master.

Every Good Gift and Every Perfect Gift Is From Above, and Cometh Down From the Father of Lights (James 1: 17)

Whether I recognize it or not, it is a fact that my possessions, my life, my talents, my abilities, my opportunities, my influence, and my life itself are God-given. How eagerly we would boast of being "self-made"! I may attribute my possessions and abilities to personal effort, drive, cunning, persistence, good fortune, or whatever; yet the Scriptural fact remains that every good gift comes from God. These statements are not to be overlooked.

God Is Not a Beggar

It is a fact that the almighty God of heaven and

[12]

earth is not poor and needy and one to whom, if so inclined, *I* may *give* from my store. Does it not seem ridiculous on the fact of it that *I*, a human being, *could* give anything material to the great God of the universe? I can give Him my love, appreciation, thanks, and loyalty. The idea of *giving* to God has become so intrenched and ingrained in our thinking and terminology, in our procedure and actual practice that it has entirely obscured the real truth. We go out helping to assemble funds for some really Christian enterprise and we are prone to say, "I am out begging." In shame we should resolve never to use such a term when so engaged, nor should we allow it to be used in our presence without protest. God is not a beggar. The nearest He comes to begging is when He *beseeches* us, for our own sakes, to repent and accept forgiveness and salvation through Christ. The terms "begging" and "giving" should be forever eliminated from our tongues and from our thinking.

A Startling Fact

It is a rather startling fact that I shall render account in the judgement day for the deeds done in the body. "So then every one of us shall give account of himself to God" (Romans 14: 12). It is hardly conceivable that, as Christians, our stewardship of time, talent, influence, and possessions should be omitted from this account. This account will be given before the throne of God and will be our *final* account.

A Member of Christ's Body

Just as my hands, my feet, and my brain are members of my body, each to serve its purpose, so am I. a member of Christ's body. "Now ye are the body of Christ, and members in particular" (1 Corinthians 12: 27). As a member of His body, that is, as a Christian, I am entitled to expect the blessings and rewards of forgiveness and eternal life. "The Son of man is come to seek and to save that which was lost" (Luke 19: 10). But we read as recorded by John where Jesus, speaking to His disciples, also said, "As my Father hath sent me, even so send I you" (John 20: 21). "Go ye therefore, and teach all nations" (Matthew 28: 19). This is involved in being a member of Christ's body. It involves a consecration of time, talent, means, and all that we have or all that we are.

These revealed facts and revealed eternal truths can not be overlooked by a Christian. They are to be learned and kept not only in mind but stored in our hearts as guides for our Christian lives.

QUESTIONS FOR STUDY AND TEACHING

1. Why should conclusions be based on tested facts and truths?

2. Name the four ways by which truths and facts are to be tested.

3. In what way may truths and facts differ?

4. What is the distinguishing character of a truth?

5. What is a principle?

[14]

6. What was an outstanding principle of Jesus?

7. Give an example of a revealed truth that is basic to all our relations to God.

8. How will a heart acceptance of this basic truth assist our understanding of the teachings of Christ and the New Testament?

9. Why would you say that our possessions of earthly goods and human ability for service are but temporary?

10. Quote a Scripture to show that not only our possessions but also we ourselves belong to God and Christ.

11. From whence do all good and perfect gifts come?

12. Why is it unthinkable that we could give to God?

13. What will be included in our final accounting?

14. What is involved in our being a member of Christ's body?

MISCONCEPTIONS TO BE ELIMINATED

Purpose of This Lesson

As Lesson One was devoted to the discovery of truths to be relied upon as guides, lesson two will be devoted to an attempt to eliminate and eradicate false and unworthy conceptions that have grown up through the centuries. These have taken such firm root that it almost is impossible for us to think in terms that really portray Christ's and the New Testament conception of the Christian's part, place, and share in the mighty works of God. Perhaps it will encourage the student if the author of this text frankly admits, at this stage, that he has a continuous struggle to try to avoid the terms and conceptions which he would, if possible, wholly eliminate in order to present the matter of our relation to God's work on an entirely different and higher plane than the most generally used terms suggest. We shall in this lesson, list six of the most common misconceptions of our stewardship of that which is God's. These generally diffused conceptions throw us off the track in attempting to portray the higher New Testament conception. They obscure the divine light.

The Idea That We Give to God

The first unworthy conception is the one most commonly held: that what we put into or appropriate to the church and Christian work is a *gift* to God. This we have mentioned in the preceding lesson but repeat here because it is so common, unworthy, and remote from the truth as to our financial and personal relation to the great God of heaven and to the Christ, the Son of the living God. Again, let us stop to consider how really ridiculous it is, after all, that we should presume to give of this world's goods and our mortal abilities to the almighty God who is the owner of the universe. The words *gift* and *giving* should be wholly eliminated from our tongues and our thinking. How the angels of God must smile, or weep, when we use these terms referring to what passes from our hands to that which we recognize as God's work.

That God Needs to Beg

The attitude that, when presenting to people the opportunity to share in the work of the "church of the living God," we allow the effort to appear as "begging" is the most unworthy of all. That is a more offensive term than *giving*. Let us repeat, for the greatest possible emphasis, that *God is no mendicant*. Let us for ever eschew such an idea. No wonder people cast in pennies as though to a panhandler. I may *give* to a tramp or any other human being, but not to God. A local congregation in a community may be needy or in financial straits and out of sympathy I may render help, but let us remember that the church is God's and Christ's. The fact of its being needy is not God's fault nor is it due to His poverty, but is the fault of God's people, who spend for earthly, and often for quite unnecessary things, that which should rightly be used in order that the cause of Christ should not appear as a mere receiver of alms.

As a Rescuer of God's Cause

Another untrue and unworthy conception is that God's will and God's work in the world would wane and perish were it not for our lending a sustaining hand. Often it may look to our human eyes as if this were true. It again suggests the same idea as that contained in these other attitudes mentioned. The chances are that God will find a way or that some one else will rise up where I fail and that God's work will go on. Since the time when Christ walked the earth it has seemed that God has never desired that the church should outshine earthly monarchies in royal wealth and splendor. Many times an apparently poor and struggling congregation can gain the hearing and attention of many people who would shy away from splendor. God's aim is at the hearts of men—all kinds of men. So long as the healing gospel of Christ is proclaimed, God's purpose is being fulfilled. It may be that God needs some poor churches. This suggestion, however, is not intended as an excuse for withholding from God's work that which is His. The only danger of too much wealth lies in its being unworthily spent in one quarter to the utter neglect of other quarters. (This matter will be treated later.)

A Debt I Owe to God

Granted that I owe everything to God, yet it is beside the point to conceive that by setting aside some fixed amount or proportion that is His by right, and which I have withheld, I can liquidate my obligation to Him by paying this amount. Again, are we willing to concede that it is merely so much money or goods that God wants of us? Are we willing to concede that we can *pay* God with money or goods? This yet falls far short of the conception of our Christian relation to God as presented in the New Testament. There is this to be said, however, that systematic and proportionate allotting is a beginning approach to a recognition that not all we may possess is exclusively our own. More and more people are adopting some such systematic plan and we may hope that it is the opening of a window to a broader and wider vision.

That the Church Is a Valuable Social Institution That Deserves Our Support by Gifts

There is a fairly widespread notion that the church is merely *one* among a number of good institutions that deserve my *patronage*. This position completely misses the point as to what the church is, whose it is, and that in its mission and purpose it has no parallel. The church of Christ is entirely different from any and all other institutions on earth. It is unique in origin, ownership, purpose, and value to man. It is the *only* institution on earth that is divine in origin. It is the *only* institu-

[19]

tion of which the Son of the almighty God is the founder and head. It is Christ's body on earth. It is the one authorized proclaimer of the gospel of Christ, which is the power of God unto salvation. It is the *one* soul-saving institution. Being divine and owned wholly by Christ, our reason for being in it and participating in its opening is, or should be, different from our participation in any other cause or institution.

Forgiveness and Salvation Can Not Be Bought

There are some who seem to think that by contributions of money they are *buying* the right to forgiveness and eternal life. Salvation from sin and death can not be bought with coins of our earthly realm. Whether the contributions be large or small, systematic or unsystematic, the fact remains that what we appropriate to the work of God, Christ, and the church must be on a different basis. This we shall seek for in the following lessons.

Summary of This Lesson

In Lesson Two we have dealt only with negatives. We have sought to clear the air of most of the usual misconceptions as to why God plans for us to participate in the one cause in which He is interested for mankind. Thus we may prepare an approach to the New Testament ideal for followers of Christ. "The Lord is not slack concerning his promise, as some men count slackness; but is longsuffering to us-ward, not willing that any should perish, but that all should come to repentance" (2 Peter 3: 9).

QUESTIONS FOR STUDY AND TEACHING

1. What is the purpose of Lesson Two?

2. Why should the word "give" not be applied to what we designate to God's work?

3. Why should the word or idea of begging never be associated with our solicitation of funds for the church and Christian work?

4. Is God's work in the world something that is dependent upon our sympathy and aid?

5. Where lies the power of God's work, in its earthly display or in its divine message?

6. What is God's chief interest in mankind?

7. Is it possible for me to liquidate what I owe to God by contributions of earthly means?

8. Why should my reason for contributions to the church be entirely different from my contributions to any other institution?

9. Name a number of characteristics of the church that are not found anywhere else.

10. Can salvation be bought by contributions large or small?

11. Why should we try to divest ourselves of the popular misconceptions about our stewardship?

CHAPTER THREE

A TRUE CONCEPTION OF THE RELATION OF A CHRISTIAN TO HIS POSSESSIONS AND TO HIS LORD

A Needed Distinction

Before we attempt to discover a true, Scriptural, and spiritual attitude, conception, and program for our Christian stewardship, let us make a clear distinction between *possession* and *ownership*. For example, a thief who steals my watch may be in possession of it, but he does not own it. The servants in Christ's parable of the servants or stewards and pounds (Luke 19: 12) were in possession of the money but did not own it. They were responsible for safeguarding the money, for using it for the benefit of the master, and for returning it. The stewards could not make restitution by returning a fixed portion, whatever that portion might be. They must account for the whole of it. The master's reward followed. Also the parable of the talents as related by Matthew 25: 14 gives us a lead on the true angle of our present possession of a bit of God's world.

Four Prevailing Conceptions

There are four predominating conceptions of possessions. They are:

1. *That what I possess is my own.* I may think that I not only *possess* but *own* what comes to my

[22]

hand, because my possessions were gained by my energy, diligence, and acumen or by that of my forefathers. These possessions being mine, I may dispose of them exactly as I see fit; I may keep or invest. The increase also is mine. I may, if I choose, *give* a portion at times to the church of Christ or any Christian work or charity, or I may cling to it all until death takes it away from me. Even then I may designate its disposal. All this is entirely legal, but does it fit the plan of God and of my Master, Christ, since it wholly disregards the first of the revealed truths about this world and its goods?

2. *That the church is one of the worthy enterprises.* I may think that the church of Christ and its many enterprises constitute *one of a number* of good and worthy causes or influences striving for a better world and therefore deserves some sympathy and support from me. I may therefore *give* as I see fit, any amount, small or large, as I may decide and as the need appears.

This is perhaps the most generally accepted and widely practiced procedure of the four mentioned in this lesson. At least it is so with the sympathetic non-church member and the nominal Christian.

Such contributions are yet counted as *gifts* and classed as *charity*. Does the almighty God seek or need charity?

3. *That part of my possessions are really God's.* I may conclude that not all of what I possess or gain is my own but that some definite part, such as one-tenth (a tithe), actually *belongs* to God, and should

be conscientiously conserved, laid by and turned over to Him, mainly through the church or congretional channels. There is this to be said for this conception at least: it is an approach toward the recognition of God's ownership. (As this will be treated later, we merely enumerate it here.)

4. *That God really owns His world.* I may come to recognize that "the earth is the Lord's, and the fulness thereof; the world, and they that dwell therein." As a Christian, I am, in a very peculiar sense, His. I am but the temporary possessor of a portion of God's earth which includes not only material wealth, but human talent, energy, and service. As a steward or trustee for God, I am permitted the rare *privilege* of partnership with Him in His blessing, uplifting, and saving the eternal souls of God's earthly children during my all too brief sojourn on earth. God has trusted me and given me this unmeasurable privilege of *partnership* with Him and expects me, as a follower of His Son, to use my possessions, my talents, and abilities to the end which is God's chiefest aim for man. "We then, as workers together with him, beseech you also that ye receive not the grace of God in vain" (2 Corinthians 6: 1).

THE PRIVILEGE OF PARTNERSHIP

God's Chiefest Blessing

The conception of a life of partnership with God raises man to the highest point of dignity and honor. Recall that man was created "a little lower than the angels." In this participating partnership my *all* is included, not money or goods or possessions alone, but my talent, my influence, my love, my loyalty, and my service in every way possible. This conception does not hint of *giving* to God nor of legal obligation of, nor of *debt* that can be liquidated by money. It is *God's chiefest blessing,* bestowed as a privilege.

A Privilege That Has Its Reward

If I thank God for this privilege of being a fellow worker with Him, and if I avail myself of the *privilege,* there is no blessing that God can bestow that is not contained in His promise for this life and that to come. The happy life here is not necessarily the life steeped in possessions, but the life filled with satisfactions that satisfy the heart of man and fade not. The consciousness here, of being a worker with God, bring life's keenest and most enduring satisfaction.

A Question That Arises

In any practical mind, this question naturally arises: If God is the owner of all and I am but a temporary steward or trustee of whatever I may possess in wealth, talent, and time, how shall I live, care for my famliy, and house, feed, clothe, and educate them? How shall I do what would appear to be a Christian's part as a citizen?

The answer lies in clearing away a false distinction we have made between what is *sacred* and what we have looked upon as *secular*. God planned the *home here* as well as *heaven there*. The Scriptures give a number of answers of which two will probably suffice: "But if any provide not for his own, and specially for those of his own house, he hath denied the faith, and is worse than an infidel" (1 Timothy 5: 8). As a citizen I am to "Render therefore unto Caesar the things that are Caesar's; and unto God the things that are God's (Matthew 22: 21). Here is provided for the exercise of our best Christian judgment and Christian conscience in acting as stewards of God's world.

All that is good and right is of God. The energy spent by the teacher, the plowman, the Christian poet, painter, or lawyer can be a part of God's plan for His people in this world. Would we say that the untiring work of a Christian mother and home-maker is not a *sacred* task of service smiled upon by the heavenly Father? The father that toils to furnish the money to feed, clothe, educate, and rear his children is definitely working under God's plan for the home. Here is a good place to add that the father not only owes it to his children to furnish the funds, but does he not owe some of his *time* and *talent* as a companion to his children?

We have too much obscured the closeness and beauty of our human relationship to God by drawing an imaginary line of segregation, ruling out as service to God or as participation and partnership with God, anything that is not a direct money or time contribution to the enterprises of the church.

[26]

Any good deed done in the name of Christ is a part of our partnership with God.

Fellowship With God

In Acts 2: 42 we read "And they [the Christians] continued stedfastly in the apostles' doctrine and fellowship, and in breaking of bread, and in prayers." Our fellowship (partnership) is not only with each other but with God. The apostles' doctrine and teaching was not confined to the assembly alone as we too much do today. "Therefore they [the disciples] that were scattered abroad went every where preaching the word." Was this not co-operation, fellowship, partnership with God and a service of stewardship for Him?

The breaking of bread was no doubt at the center of their worship periods in their assemblies. We learn further in the Scriptures that prayer was by no means confined to the assembly. Quite apparently from many references and suggestions in the Scriptures, daily prayers, private prayers, family prayer, prayer for others, as well as prayer in the assembly, was a constant and prominent feature. This keeping of the altar fires of prayer burning was a part of the carrying out of their stewardship, quite as much as their laying by in store when they assembled.

A Prominent Factor in the Fellowship

The *fellowship* was as much a definite part of New Testament worship as was the *preaching, break-*

ing of bread, and *prayers* (see Acts 2: 42). This fellowship was much more indeed than mere social fraternity and mutual Christian association. Its real meaning is *partnership* with each other and with God in the Lord's work. The Christian farmer, the goldsmith, the scribe, the shopkeeper, and all others of divers trades and professions, each cast into the treasury. The funds thus gained by differing people in differing ways and differing abilities became *one* fund consecrated to the work of God. It was a fellowship, a partnership fund. Thus they had fellowship with each other and with God. Note that this *fellowship* is one of the *four* features of New Testament worship. Our setting aside of money together with other Christians is as *sacred* and Christian as any other of the four features of worship. It should be done not as a *gift,* nor payment nor fulfillment of legal requirement, but with the same spirit of consecration and reverence as is given to the teaching of the apostles' doctrine, the breaking of bread, or the prayers. It should be as conscientiously, faithfully, and regularly done as are these other features of the New Testament church which are revealed to us in Acts 2: 42.

The contributing of money should never be done in the spirit of payment of a debt, the support of a needy God, nor as a mundane and mercenary but necessary feature of our membership in Christ's church. It is a reverent part of New Testament described worship and will be done willingly and cheerfully by Christians.

[28]

The Spirit in Which We Contribute

The spirit in which we contribute money for the work of the church is to be considered. The consciousness of partnership and fellowship with God will very materially change the spirit in which we contribute. God knows the spirit as well as the act. We might contribute regularly and even what is called generously and yet grudgingly. Such a spirit can easily accompany the idea that we are *giving* to God or to Christ's church, but it will not accompany the attitude of partnership or fellowship with God. A right spirit multiplies our joy and thus becomes an earnest of our reward as a steward.

Marching With the Redeemed

As a *partner* we join a mighty host of both the living and those who have gone before. We become real sharers and participants in the most worthwhile, worthy, and notable enterprise on earth, with Christ as our captain and God as our partner. We are marching with that joyous throng, the ranks of the redeemed, and sharing in making the kingdoms of this world the kingdom of our Lord. What we are able to do is done, not of necessity, nor of law, but as a voluntary participation because we love Him who loved us enough to die for us.

QUESTIONS FOR STUDY AND TEACHING

1. Explain and illustrate the difference between *possession* and *ownership*.

2. What is the generally accepted conception of

our relation to all of the things which we possess?

3. How does this conception contradict the great basic principle of God's ownership?

4. Is the church of Christ merely one of a number of good and worthy enterprises in the world? How does it stand out as entirely different?

5. Where is the error in classing our contributions to the work of the church as a charity?

6. Name one method of contribution that is at least an approach to the recognition of God's ownership of all.

7. What is the true and Scriptural conception of our relationship to God as concerning our possession of means, time, and talent?

8. Should stewardship be considered as a duty, obligation, or privilege?

9. How does real stewardship lift one in dignity?

10. What rewards are assured for our partnership with God?

11. If all is God's, how is the Christian to take care of family and citizenship obligations?

12. Is the care of earthly relationships sacred or purely earthly?

13. Name some of the ways in which the early Christians fellowshiped with God.

14. In what spirit should we make our contributions?

STEWARDSHIP AND SPIRITUAL GROWTH

A Characteristic of Humanity

Now and through all recorded time, a noticeable trait of man has been the unbreakable connection between his possessions and his interests. Jesus put it tersely in the Sermon on the Mount, "Where your treasure is, there will your heart be also" (Matthew 6: 21). This follows His preceding warning in verses 19, 20, in which He urged His disciples to "Lay not up for yourselves treasures upon earth, where moth and rust doth corrupt, and where thieves break through and steal: but lay up for yourselves treasures in heaven, where neither moth nor rust doth corrupt, and where thieves do not break through nor steal." This same thought is presented vividly in the parable of the rich fool (Luke 12: 15).

Not only does true stewardship mean a laying up for the eternal future, but the best and surest way to fix the heart on God and things eternal is to put treasure, effort, and time into the works of God.

An illustrative story is told of a small boy who was a member of a large Bible school. His teacher missed him one Sunday, and on the next Sunday he saw the boy passing by the church house. When the teacher asked where he was going, he replied, "I'm going down to that little mission Sunday school. I was down there last Sunday and gave them a dime.

[31]

I'm going down to see what they did with it." This simple story will illustrate a universal phase of human psychology. "Where your treasure is, there will your heart be also." Perhaps here is God's reason for taking us into partnership. It is the heart of man that God wants, and this is one way to win man's heart.

The word *heart* as used here, and in a number of other places in the New Testament, includes the *intellect, feelings* such as interest, affection, etc., and the *will*. The whole problem of the relation of man to God as revealed in both the Old and the New Testaments is to get man to give to God his heart, fully, freely, and permanently. If this is achieved then all is achieved. Problems of obedience, loyalty, stewardship, uprightness, all will be solved.

A Fact Demonstrated

Here would be a good place to remind ourselves of an established fact, proved and demonstrated through all time and history of man. It is this: with all the effort, striving, contentions, wars, bickering, and bloodshed that have resulted from man's struggles to amass wealth, there is not one record among all the millions where it has satisfied the souls of those who succeeded in the struggle. History's pages are packed with records of ennui, unsatisfied longings, heart-hunger, disappointment, and disillusionment of worldly successful men, who have missed God, Christ, and heaven because their hearts were where their treasures were, i. e., in things of this world. While this is not an argument taken from the New Testament, yet it is a startling fact proved by universal experience, and facts must be taken into account. Quite probably the poor widow who cast her two mites, which was her all, into the treasury, received more joy and lasting satisfaction out of it than any Midas has ever known.

Man's Most Tragic Mistake

The teachings of Jesus point out most strikingly the most serious and tragic mistake any soul can make in this life. He put it this way: "What shall it profit a man, if he shall gain the whole world, and lose his own soul? Or what shall a man give in exchange for his soul?" (Mark 8: 36, 37). This statement is preceded by one quite as striking: "For whosoever shall save his life shall lose it; but whosover will lose his life for my sake and the gospel's, the same shall save it" (Verse 35). This again is preceded by a kindred teaching, "Whosoever will come after me, let him deny himself, and take up his cross, and follow me" (Verse 34).

The parables of the talents and pounds also enforce the same thought. As Christians we have accepted Christ not only as the *Saviour* and Son of God, but as *Lord* and *Master* as well. Do we really believe what He has said?

Real Stewardship Is a Most Practical Help in Soul Growth

Not only are we to accept, acknowledge, and obey Christ as our Saviour, but we are to *live* in

[33]

Him and *for* Him. We are to go forward. We are to "grow in grace and knowledge of the truth." For a child to be born and never grow at all is as sad and serious as death. The New Testament not only tells us *how to become* Christians, centering that information largely in the Book of Acts, but it gives us twenty-one books—the Epistles—to tell us *how to live as Christians.* This is in addition to the foundation principles of Christian discipleship as taught by Jesus and recorded in the Gospels. Then there is the final warning in the final book of the New Testament, Revelation, the burden of which is contained in one verse, "Be thou faithful unto death, and I will give thee a crown of life" (Revelation 2: 10). Also in the closing words of the Book of books, the Word of God, we read, "Behold, I come quickly; and my reward is with me, to give every man according as his work shall be" (Revelation 22: 12), and in verse 14, "Blessed are they that do his commandments, that they may have right in the tree of life, and may enter in through the gates into the city."

Where Stewardship Comes In

Through stewardship, God graciously made it possible for mortal men to use simple, earthly things and abilities at our hands as the surest means of growth in Christ. Thus we fix our hope in Him, we confirm our faith in Him, and we strengthen our resolve to be faithful unto death that where He is, there may we be. To grow is the best assurance

[34]

of continued life. We grow, not by what we plan to do but by what we do.

QUESTIONS FOR STUDY AND TEACHING

1. How did Jesus make plain our need to share in God's work?

2. How is stewardship a best help toward fixing our lives toward God?

3. Has the amassing of earthly wealth ever satisfied the soul of any man?

4. What is or can be man's most tragic mistake?

5. What did Jesus say about it though we should gain the whole world?

6. Name some parables that illustrate the points in the preceding question.

7. How does stewardship contribute to soul growth?

8. How is God's reward related to our acts?

9. How did God plan to make it possible for us to use our earthly means and abilities to draw us to Him?

OUR CONCEPTION OF OUR SHARE IN GOD'S WORK SHOULD COME FROM THE NEW TESTAMENT

We Now Live Under the New Testament, Not the Old; Under the Christian Dispensation, Not the Patriarchal or Mosaic

It is generally agreed by most great Christian groups that we are now living under the New Testament, as our divine guide, and not under the Old Testament. We may recall the Scripture which reads, "Wherefore the law [referring to the Old Testament] was our schoolmaster to bring us unto Christ, that we might be justified by faith. But after that faith is come, we are no longer under a schoolmaster" (Galatians 3: 24, 25); or again, "Blotting out the handwriting of ordinances that was against us, which was contrary to us, and took it out of the way, nailing it to his cross" (Colossians 2: 14).

These inspired statements, given by the apostle Paul, make it plain that the dispensation of the law ended at the cross. We now live not under the law, but under Christ; not in the patriarchal or Mosaic dispensation but in the Christian dispensation under the gospel. The New Testament is the guide and mentor for the Christian dispensation. To it we must go for guidance in Christian procedure and duty.

[36]

A student of the Bible can plainly see that the New Testament holds up standards in all phases of man's relation to God that are much higher than the standards of the Old Testament. Christ made it plain that, "All power is given unto me in heaven and in earth" (Matthew 28: 18). In the early part of the Sermon on the Mount we find Jesus saying, "Ye have heard that it was said by them of old time . . . but I say unto you . . ." (Matthew 5:21-37); and here He quotes law after law of the Old Testament, and follows each with the Christian principle of the New Testament.

The New Testament Is Sufficient to All Christian Purposes

The New Testament furnishes all needed guidance and instruction. It, in its logical arrangement, gives complete and divinely inspired instruction for all procedures necessary to salvation. It provides for the exercise of consecrated judgment in many of the problems that face us, but in all basic matters it is complete and sufficient. "All scripture is given by inspiration of God, and is profitable for doctrine, for reproof, for correction, for instruction in righteousness: that the man of God may be perfect, throughly furnished unto all good works" (2 Timothy 3: 16, 17). Nothing more is needed. The one thing needed is that followers of Christ know the New Testament Scriptures and commit themselves to the principles there presented. Thus may we "grow in grace, and in the knowledge of our Lord and Saviour Jesus Christ," "Till we all

[37]

come in the unity of the faith, and of the knowledge of the Son of God, unto a perfect man, unto the measure of the stature of the fulness of Christ" (2 Peter 3: 18 and Ephesians 4: 13).

A Source of Confusion

The failure to recognize the New Testament as the *one* divinely given guide for Christian life opens the gate for the entry of much sectarian difference and confusion of teaching. It also is an invitation to enemies and critics of the Bible to offer what appears to be glaring contradictions in the Bible. Ingersoll said, "The Bible is full of contradictions, and I can prove it in a minute." Then he proceeded to quote passages from the Old Testament and set over against them passages from the New which appeared to be contradictory. They seemingly were contradictions, unless one understands that the Old Testament has been superseded as an authoritative guide by the later will of God as revealed by Christ and the New Testament. Understanding this fact at once sweeps away any such blatant and boastful criticism made by Ingersoll or any other like him.

The Plan of The New Testament

The plan of the New Testament is logical and complete.

1. The four Gospels present the *evidence that Jesus is the Christ, the Son of the living God*. They also give us what we have of the teachings of Jesus in which He laid down the basic principles of the

[38]

Christian life. This evidence is full and conclusive and, as John says, "These are written, that ye might believe that Jesus is the Christ, the Son of God; and that believing ye might have life through his name." Here are given the facts that should lead every man to want to be a Christian and lead him to ask the question, "What shall I do?"

2. The question, "What shall we do to be saved?" is answered mainly in one book, the Book of Acts. (See Acts 2: 37, 38.) This book furnishes the answer to this question for all people in all places in all times.

3. To those who accept Him as Saviour and obey Him as Lord, in other words, to those who become Christians there are given twenty-one books (the Epistles) to cover all phases, problems, duties, and procedures needed to guide Christian life and practice.

4. The wonderful volume closes with the Book of Revelation, which looks forward through prophecy to the final days of earth and to the judgment day. The burden of its message, is: "Be thou faithful unto death, and I will give thee a crown of life" (Revelation 2: 10). The New Testament covers everything from our being begotten anew through the gospel (1 Corinthians 4: 15) and our being born into the kingdom of Christ (John 3: 4-8), and on through the whole of life and unto the judgment day after death. Thus is its coverage complete. Could it be that God has overlooked any needed thing for us?

[39]

A Distinctive Feature of the New Testament Presentation

In the early days, in the childhood of the races, God dealt even with His chosen people as children. The law was first given and appears in the form of "Thou shalt" and "Thou shalt not." Thus we deal with little children lest they destroy themselves. As people become grown they are and must be guided by principles which have been instilled in their lives. The New Testament is based on *principles*. That God is the Supreme Ruler of the universe is a principle. Love for God and Christ is a principle by which almost any specific question or problem can be answered and solved. Loyalty and service are principles under which a thousand questions, doubts, and problems can be solved. Some Christian bodies have attempted to write into creedal laws and church rules many "thou shalts" and "shalt nots"; but the New Testament procedure is to establish faith, obedience in heart and action, loyalty, and love. The individual is expected to adopt practices in keeping with these principles. God does not *force* us. He would lead us, having given all needed principles for our guidance. This applies to our stewardship as well as to many problems of Christian life, service, and conduct.

QUESTIONS FOR STUDY AND TEACHING

1. Under what dispensation do we now live?

2. Where do we find the divine guidance and instruction for Christians?

3. Does the New Testament give all needed and sufficient guidance?

4. Quote a Scripture stating the fact of the above question.

5. What is our chief need as to this instruction?

6. How does a failure to recognize the distinction between the Old and the New Testaments lay the ground for confusion and carping criticism?

7. Outline the plan of the New Testament.

8. What is a distinctive feature of the New Testament as compared with the Old?

9. How do you account for God giving us a *new* will after the coming of Christ?

A CRYING NEED FOR NEW TESTAMENT TEACHING ON OUR MONETARY AND SERVICE RELATIONS TO GOD

The Incident of the Pentecost Disciples

The three thousand who accepted Christ as Saviour and openly obeyed Him as Lord on Pentecost, plus the fifteen thousand others shortly added to them in Jerusalem, were so thrilled with joy and appreciation of what Christ meant to them that without particular instruction they voluntarily sold their possessions and laid the proceeds at the apostles' feet. This was done without orders from any source. Had it been done by request or orders from the apostles, we would be compelled to consider it an apostolic precedent for all other Christian groups in all other places and times. However, we have no New Testament record of this procedure being followed in any other place under apostolic guidance. We may conclude that this was an incident and not a precedent. We do find this statement in Acts 4: 32: "Neither said any of them that ought of the things which he possessed was his own; but they had all things common." Some have tried to make this a precedent for political socialism or for so-called Christian communism. We must understand the difference. Communism is a political doctrine by which the individual is compelled to place his all at the dictum and disposal of the politi-

cal power. Communism is enforced from the top
down and it is compulsory. This incident in Jerusalem was from the bottom up and was wholly voluntary. There is no New Testament record of
the continuance of the practice. Today, any Christian group could do the same as a *voluntary* act,
but there is no New Testament command or precedent that would call for it. We consider this incident here because it is one of the New Testament
incidents where money is involved. It is at least a
challenging example of the appreciation which these
disciples had for what Christ and the gospel meant
to them.

A Bit of Church History

Since Pentecost there have been, according to
the best possible estimates, seven and a half billions
of people who accepted Christ as Saviour. There
are now living about six hundred millions of people in many lands who acknowledge Christ as Lord.
This includes all groups, sects, and denominations.

In the Dark Ages there were no Bibles available
to the people and almost none for priests and teachers. Ambitious men became the top leaders and
dominated the rapidly spreading church. These men
waged many actual wars for control and power.
Many kinds of practices, contrary to both the spirit
and letter of the teachings of Christ and the New
Testament, were introduced in the organizations
which occupied the place in the minds, hearts, and
lives of the people that was once held by the simple

and spiritual New Testament church of Christ.

Among these extra-Scriptural and anti-Scriptural practices there were adopted innumerable kinds of un-Christian and even vicious schemes to get money to aggrandize the leading clergy and feed their ambition for power and display. The clergy even went to the extreme of peddling, for money, the right to commit any kind of sin or crime one might desire to commit, the clergy agreeing to see that the sinners' crimes were absolved. This is recorded here merely to show how Christian stewardship was prostituted and replaced by collections, charges for priestly service, and every conceivable kind of money-raising device. Protestantism grew from a revolt against such practices.

The Reaction of Protestantism

Protestantism reacted against this ungodly system and these departures from New Testament spirit and practice. Naturally, every radical action begets an extreme reaction. Thus it was that Protestantism shied away from these un-Christian tactics but in turn went to the extreme of practically ignoring a real Christian stewardship. "Salvation is free" was misinterpreted and overworked. Since the minister's living came from members of the church he had the greatest reticence about even mentioning any matter involving money. The result was an almost entire neglect of teaching the principles of Christian stewardship and related principle that "Where your treasure is, there will your heart be also." One of the greatest services that could be rendered to the great host of Christians would be to teach them the stewardship of money, time, and talent. It is also true that one of the surest ways to arouse and cultivate the interest of those who have not yet accepted Christ as Saviour is to tactfully induce them to put something into the work of Christ.

Faith Cometh by Hearing, and Hearing by the Word of God

Not only does *faith* come by hearing the Word of God, but in turn every Christian virtue and means of grace and growth comes in exactly the same way. Human minds react in the same psychological way. There is a definite, natural sequence which can be listed as *hearing*: conviction or believing, resolution, action, growth. This is the true order in the Scriptural plan of salvation, i. e., teaching people to accept Christ and then in teaching them to grow Christian virtues and practices. "Teach . . . baptize . . . teach."

Popular Tactics Often Used

Slogans, drives, catch phrases, competitions, and like devices may promote the *giving* of money, either reluctantly or gladly, but in such cases the response is temporary. These methods lack much indeed of the Scriptural ideal in which the Christian is led to a conviction of his stewardship of God's substance, and out of this conviction he voluntarily and systematically shares his means, talent,

[45]

and life in God's work. In speaking of God's work we must recall that it does not all take place in the church house on Sunday. It is a seven-day-a-week work, wherever the Christian may go. Every tendency to avoid plain teaching or the absolute necessity for sharing as a partner with God in all God's work and all reticence on the part of proclaimers of the gospel and teachers should for ever be put aside.

Where Do We Get Our Ideas and Practices As to Our Contributions?

It is almost entirely by observation of the practices of others that most of us get our ideas. If as new Christians we observe elders and older Christians fishing out a shiny dime on Sunday to toss into a *collection* basket, we are very likely to conclude that that is what we should do. We may have spent ten dollars on Saturday evening for pleasure or some entirely unnecessary thing.

Is there not a better way to decide on what a Christian's stewardship would suggest? Is there no better way than simply to ape the practices of people wholly untaught as to a Christian's stewardship?

Education in Christian Principles Needed

The answer to the questions raised in the preceding paragraph is in education from the spirit and letter of the Scriptures.

1. *Where should education in stewardship begin?* Where and when in life should education for stewardship begin? Our answer is, "From the first time a little child asks the question, 'Where did I come

from?' and we answer, 'God made you.' This child grows up with this fact fixed. He asks, 'Where did the world come from?' We answer, 'God made the world and the trees, and grass, the flowers, and everything.'" Why not add a bit more and there and then begin planting the truth that God not only made the world and everything in it, and that it is God's world, that it is all His, but that He lets us use and take care of His world for Him while we are here.

2. *Next Step in Teaching.* The Bible school is the next added opportunity to enforce the truth as to God's world. Why not train our teachers of the younger children to teach that not only did God make the world and all in it, but that God owns it and lends it to us while we are here, so we may have bread and fruit to eat, cotton and wool to make our clothes, and wood, steel, and stone to build our homes and a thousand needed and beautiful buildings, roads and bridges, and that it is yet God's? Let us plant early the Scriptural idea that, "Every good gift . . . is from above, and cometh down from the Father of lights." These truths implanted in the mind during early childhood will help to direct both mind and heart to the great and eternal truth so much overlooked.

3. *For Older Pupils and Adults.* Here is the time to fasten the ideas by practice. This is to be done by instruction, example, and attitude. If this *is* God's world, does He expect us to use it only or almost entirely for our own good and pleasure?

Teach the difference between *possessorship* and *ownership* on our part. Teach the principle of stewardship, i. e. *partnership* with God.

4. *The Minister's Part in Teaching Stewardship.* The time has long been overdue for ministers to put aside false modesty and reticence. Is it not as much the duty of the minister to teach New Testament principles on what is comprehended in *Christian life and living* as to teach the primary steps in *becoming* a Christian? Care should be taken to leave no misapprehension as to the minister's motives. To leave any impression that he is a mere promotional agent, a money-raiser for this or that, should be avoided carefully. He should ever keep in mind that God is interested only in the souls of men and that sharing our lives and possessions is merely one of God's means of calling and holding us to Him. We should ever try to make this clear. Our contributions are not because of God's need but of our need.

To appear as only the mercenary agent for some enterprise, agency, or scheme is not conducive to the development of the principle of permanent Christian stewardship. Let the minister, without excuse or apology, frankly teach the Christian's partnership with God as a matter of conscience on his part, "Teach . . . baptize . . . teach" (See Matthew 28: 18-20).

A Reiteration

This lesson is to close with a repetition of the statement with which it began. The most crying need as to Christian stewardship is for plain and abundant Scriptural teaching on the subject. It is easier to pronounce a specific and plain law than it is to instill a principle. God, though basing Old Testament teaching and practice on definite laws, saw fit, through Christ and the Holy Spirit, to base Christianity and its practices on principles, leaving Christians to adopt them. The principle of God's ownership of all, if absorbed in mind and heart, will lead to a life of consecrated Christian stewardship.

QUESTIONS FOR STUDY AND TEACHING

1. Would you say that the incident of the Pentecost contributions is given as a precedent for all Christians in all time?

2. Distinguish between their act and the principles of modern communism.

3. Why is there a crying need for abundant and plain *New Testament* teachings on the matter of stewardship?

4. Give examples from church history showing how departures were made from the New Testament spirit and practice.

5. What were some of the un-Scriptural practices foisted upon the Christians of the early centuries?

6. What was the purpose of many of these money-gathering practices?

7. To what extremes did the then leaders of the church go?

[49]

8. How did these practices help to start Protestantism?

9. What was Protestantism's reaction?

10. How is faith or real Christian practice to be restored?

11. What are some of today's tactics for "raising funds"?

12. Where do most of us get our ideas as to what we should contribute?

13. Where and how should education in stewardship begin?

14. What steps should be taken in the Bible school?

15. What basic principle should be taught to the adult Christian?

16. What is the minister's part and duty in stewardship education?

17. Why should the minister present the matter as a distinctive feature in Christian growth rather than appearing to be a mere money-raising agent for some particular cause or agency?

18. Summarize the main idea bought out in Lesson Six.

ALLOWANCE FOR GROWTH IN OUR CHRISTIAN CONCEPTIONS

Is the High Standard of Stewardship, Here Presented, Practical?

An old presentation of the act of *becoming* a Christian was based on the idea of a cataclysmic, sudden, and revolutionary change. It was termed "getting religion." The new Christian was presumed to explode into the seventh heaven of perfection immediately.

This is not what is outlined and portrayed in the New Testament. Rather it presents a system of being *born* anew, being at first a *"babe"* in the kingdom and then a continuous *growth* in grace and knowledge of the truth. This growth is expected to continue to the end of life here. The New Testament provides for a growth deep enough and wide enough in spiritual insight, stability, power, and influence to lend a further challenge to even the best and most mature of Christians, so long as life shall last. When we remember this, the New Testament plan is practical indeed. Naturally, in all phases of Christian development, the *highest* standard must be held up for all the phases of Christian life and development. Truly the conception of *perfection* in Christ Jesus must be presented and kept before us as that for which we strive. It is a challenge to continued growth.

[51]

The New Birth

Jesus said, "Ye must be *born* again." There is a spiritual birth as well as a physical. (Read John 3: 1-7.) We are begotten through the gospel (1 Corinthians 4: 15), which means that through hearing the gospel the first stirrings of spiritual life are begun. This new life comes forth as a newborn babe when the acts of obedience to the gospel are completed. We emerge from the waters of Christian baptism, having buried the old man or old life, and are thus raised or born to the new life *in Christ*. Paul, in writing to the Corinthians, spoke of a newborn babe in Christ. He said, "I have fed you with milk, and not with meat: for hitherto ye were not able to bear it" (1 Corinthians 3: 2). And in another place Paul said, "For every one that useth milk is unskillful in the word of righteousness: for he is yet a babe" (Hebrews 5: 13). These Scriptures are cited to assure us that the Scriptural plan provides not only for a new birth but for babyhood and then continued growth. This sequence is true for all our development in the Christian virtues and activities.

Growth Is Epected of Us

Growth in grace and knowledge of the truth is not only emphatically set forth in the New Testament, but it is made a definite part of the whole Christian scheme. Unlike our physical growth, it does not have a fixed point at which growth practically stops and another at which decline begins, but spiritual growth is to continue so long as life shall last. Do we not all need to stop and ask ourselves, "Am I going forward or backward? Have I grown any in Christian spirit in this past year? Am I stronger or weaker, more Christlike or less? Am I more fitted to represent the Christ and serve Him than I was this time last year?"

Means of Spiritual Growth

The New Testament names, provides, and offers clear and definite means of spiritual growth. Without the use of these means, growth can not take place. The three main means are:

1. *The Word.* The apostle Peter puts it this way, "As newborn babes, desire the sincere milk of the word, that ye may grow thereby" (1 Peter 2: 2). Jesus said, "My Father giveth you the true bread from heaven. For the bread of God is he which cometh down from heaven, and giveth life unto the world . . . and Jesus said unto them, I am the bread of life" (John 6: 32, 33, 35). Scriptures could be multiplied which contemplate food for life and growth. This food can be obtained in at least three ways: (1) Personally reading the Word regularly and constantly, (2) hearing the Word preached regularly, (3) hearing the Word taught regularly.

2. *Prayer.* Prayer is not merely *asking* God for things mundane or heavenly. Nor is it alone a giving of thanks. Prayer may include both of these elements. Basically, however, prayer is a coming

[53]

face to face with the heavenly Father. Study Jesus' prayers as to that fact. It is a communion with God, a talking directly to God out from the heart.

No soul can thus come sincerely face to face with God without a stimulus to growth in spiritual life. For a time the things that so largely occupy our earthly lives are shut out or obscured in the presence of God. No Christian can really and sincerely pray without uplift in Christian development.

3. *Work.* By work we mean spiritual exercise, co-operation with God. Here is where real stewardship, i.e., conscious partnership with God, comes in. In real stewardship, all the acts of our lives may be brought into play. "Whatsoever ye do in word or deed, do all in the name of the Lord Jesus" (Colossians 3: 17). How many of our acts are in His name? Whether a mother or father, a husband or wife, an employer or an employee, rich or poor, a farmer or a lawyer—whatever our calling—if our acts are tempered and shaped by being done in the name of Christ, we are working in co-operation, partnership, and stewardship with the heavenly Father. Stewardship is really a comprehensive word and certainly includes much more than the giving of money. Sharing our possessions can not be left out, but that act, by no means, covers all. It is, however, one of the chief means by which we grow in grace and knowledge of the truth.

The Christian Beginnings

Remembering that the means of growth are provided, because the newborn babe is not fully grown, both God and Christ appear to exercise the kindliest of sympathy toward God's children. Too often older Christians would demand a grown man's view and performance from the newborn. The heights have to be scaled before we can reach the top. Truly the heights must be pointed out and it must be made plain that the little child's participation is but a start. Too many remain in the Sunday-school penny-, nickel-, and dime-stage year after year. Too many absorb from the rest of us the conception of *giving to God*. From the day of the child's Sunday-school pennies, the consciousness of partnership with God and Christ must be instilled. This will lay the ground for growth in spirit and understanding of what it really means to be a Christian. The adult who becomes a Christian, frequently has to pass through this same slow process; but being mature, he can develop much more rapidly. He begins, however, as a babe in Christ, a newborn creature.

Our Christian Duty to the Newborn

On the part of ministers, teachers, Christian leaders and parents there is a clear duty toward the newborn in Christ.

1. *The Minister's Place.* The minister's first task is an uninhibited teaching of the Christian's place by the side of God in all things. False reticence as to monetary participation and service in the name of Christ should be entirely eliminated. The Christian's standards should be for ever held on high.

But all should be done sympathetically, bearing in mind that his teaching is a planting intended to take root and grow. To this may be added his example. It still remains true that most people gain their conceptions of a Christian's part and place in the plans of God from observation of others, and especially observation of the minister, the Bible teacher, and parents.

2. *The Bible Teacher's Duty.* Much the same that has been said of the minister's place in the creation of stewardship consciousness and conscience may be repeated in picturing the Bible teacher's place. However, as Bible teachers deal with different ages and grades, their presentations have to be determined by this fact.

3. *Church Leaders.* Each congregation has to choose its leadership from the best material available. Since none is perfect, leaders will not be perfect in either performance or example. However, they must be kept aware that their example and attitude is that which determines the attitude and practice of those whom they lead. It is an honor to be chosen as an elder or deacon, but it is likewise a distinct responsibility. We should all strive to help our leaders lift up their eyes to the heights that they may lead others to the heights of service, joy, and blessing.

4. *Parents and Their Duty.* It is to be kept in mind that we here are speaking of *Christian* parents. Unfortunately, it is frequently a fact that parents are themselves not members of Christ's body. In

this case the whole task falls back on the Bible teachers and ministers.

In the case of Christian parents it can be said that they are in the place of the most strategic advantage for implanting true Christian ideals and practices, but too often they waive their responsibility and delegate it to others.

Again it is a case of Bible knowledge, Bible teaching, and home practice and example. When we all stand before the great white throne, the first matter of importance will be, "What did you do about Christ?" and probably the second will be, "What did you do about the children God put in your hands?"

QUESTIONS FOR STUDY AND TEACHING

1. Is the New Testament standard for stewardship practiced or possible for us today?

2. What is God's plan as to our becoming Christians as babes in Christ, followed by growth?

3. Why must the highest and most perfect standard be held before us?

4. Whence comes the begetting or first stirring of the new birth in Christ?

5. Is a period of development and growth anticipated in the New Testament?

6. Name one difference between our physical growth and our spiritual growth.

7. How can we test ourselves?

8. What are some of the means for spiritual growth? Name three.

9. In what peculiar way does prayer help in Christian development?

10. How much ground is covered in the idea of Christian work?

11. What mistake do we often make in our expectations of newborn babes in Christ?

12. What are our stewardship duties toward the newborn? What of the minister, the church officers, the Bible-school teachers, and parents?

APPROACHES MADE TOWARD CHRISTIAN STEWARDSHIP

Our Reason for Contributions

The *reason* behind our contributions of money, time, or service is of supreme importance. Recall the offerings of Cain and Abel. Cain's offering may have been more valuable than Abel's, but it was Abel's offering that God accepted. Their attitudes toward God were the reasons.

One might contribute merely to keep up "face" with the folk round about. One might contribute merely because it has become a custom to put something into the collection basket, starting from our penny taken to Sunday school. One might contribute to be seen of men and gain their favor for business purposes. One might contribute as a salve for a guilty conscience. There probably are many similar reasons, but none of them is or even *approaches* Christian stewardship.

None of these reasons in the heart has much effect in drawing us really closer to God and developing our spirits in Christian conviction, loyalty, and stability.

The consciousness of participation in the work of God, as a partner in His work in the world, does help to shape our lives to the model comprehended for one who is "in Christ." It does draw us ever closer to Him and build us up in Christ. It is the

[59]

giver and not the gift that God greatly desires.

A Blessing and Privilege

Sharing as a partner with God is to be kept in mind as a blessed *privilege*. The value of all the following lessons depends on this basic fact, when it is absorbed and kept in mind and heart. If this is done, much light will break on the teachings of Jesus and the portrayal of the Christian life by the apostles. When we come to look upon our participation as a *privilege,* rather than as a debt paid, a fiat obeyed, an obligation fulfilled, or as a *gift* to God, then will joy be shed abroad to brighten every day of life. Its end will be transformed from a mournful entry into the dark to a glorious victory over death and a triumphant entry into the bright sunshine of God's glory.

Some Usual Methods Followed

1. *The Spasmodic Giver.* By spasmodic we mean the occasional giver. We use the term "giver" because that is the term that the contributor uses. There are two things involved here: One is that the attitude of *giving to the Almighty* is based on a wrong and un-Scriptural concept. We merely possess—not own—and therefore we can not give to Him. The earth and all therein is yet God's. The second weakness is that the giving, even if such it be, *is* spasmodic, irregular, not to be counted on and subject to human whim instead of a fixed purpose to be a true steward. A Christian's participation

in the works of God should be such a fixed part of his everyday life, every week, and every year Christian life that each day's income is shared regularly.

2. *Giving Occasionally in Response to Spellbinding Appeals.* Giving in response to heart-rending appeals is yet the idea of *"giving to God,"* but this idea should be for ever dispensed with by a Christian. Again, the motive might be any one of several that do not recognize God's ownership, nor our stewardship under Him, of what we have in means, time, and talent.

3. *Other Reasons for Giving.* In former lessons we have listed and discussed some of the false notions for appropriating of the means we possess. Among these was the false notion of *God's need, God's poverty,* etc. Such we need not discuss again here.

Systematic Giving

We still use the popular term "giving" because it is the term widely used even where the contributions become systematic and proportionate. While these methods *approach* the idea of God's ownership and our stewardship, they may lack much of a full Christian conception.

1. *Tithing as a Systematic Method.* We mention tithing because it *is* systematic and makes much the closest approach to real stewardship. It *does* recognize God's ownership of at least a part of our possessions. We should have no inclinations to criticize the thousands of godly, conscientious souls who

are regular tithers; rather, we only commend them. Tithing is the most widely practiced systematic method adopted to date because it is a partial recognition of God's ownership and does *approach* the conception of real Christian stewardship, i.e., partnership with God. It is a method, which any Christian may adopt as a *voluntary* method of sharing with Christ the task of winning the unsaved to Him. If done because of love for God, Christ, and the church, it is to be commended to the millions of Christians who have never come even that close to partnership with God and Christ.

Some Things To Be Guarded Against in Tithing

There are a number of things to be kept in mind, however, even by conscientious tithers.

1. *As a Means of Liquidating Our Debt to God.* Tithing is too often presented as the mere *paying* back to God what we *owe* Him and have withheld from Him. The feeling is very often apparent that now "I've paid God the full amount that I owe Him," when a tenth of my monetary income is devoted to work recognized as God's work, especially the church. This idea of *paying* God and liquidating the debt is not the highest, for it sometimes makes one feel that he may overlook other Christian virtues. The writer has personally known some meticulous tithers who paid their tenth on Sunday and would swear like a trooper on Monday and lie without compunction on Tuesday. No doubt the Jews who cried loudest for the blood of Christ and

demanded His crucifixion were punctilious tithers.

This is not to condemn tithing but to call attention to the fact that it is far from a payment in *full* to God. God wants the humble and contrite and loving spirit. No one should criticize tithing as a method of filling God's storehouse unless he has accepted and adopted something better and more effective.

Tithing is in no sense to be condemned because of the laxity of some tithers in other virtues any more than Christ and the church should be eschewed because of the imperfections of individual Christians. Nothing we have urged is to be counted as a criticism of tithers or tithing, but rather of the arguments presented to lead Christians to adopt tithing as a legal obligation, based on Old Testament law, giving the impression that this method is the *one,* and *only one* Scripturally sanctioned, and made a definite Christian obligation. In some cases it is made to appear as practically a fifth condition in the plan of salvation.

Tithing as a Legal Obligation

God is interested in the hearts and motives of men. In the former dispensations God dealt with man through the law. Under Christ and Christianity, He gives us broad principles based on *love.* To tithe as a matter of fulfillment of an Old Testament legal obligation, such as we are so frequently urged, is not necessarily done because of love or a sense of partnership with God, but as the *fulfillment* of a *legal obligation*. This is not the highest motive that could be the basis for Christian sharing of means, time, and talent. Again it can lead to a feeling of having fulfilled what is required, wiping out or lessening the importance of other obligations. Even regular and conscientious tithing can not be substituted for real love, devotion, and virtue.

Whatever basis, method, or plan one may use for participating personally as a partner with God, it must be one that answers God's purpose of bringing the participant closer in heart to God.

Spiritual Benefits of Tithing

With any pitfall that might beset the way of tithing it must, at the same time, be said that it has been the means of blessing and enriching the lives of those who have adopted it. May there be millions more enrolled and may those in the ranks go forward "toward the mark for the prize of the high calling of God in Christ Jesus" (Philippians 3: 14). Thus may these lead us all the vision of Christian stewardship, wherein we see our Lord and Saviour as our real leader in all the phases of our earthly life. His teaching, and that of the apostles in the New Testament, is our source of authority for our Christian life and practice.

QUESTIONS FOR STUDY AND TEACHING

1. Name some of the `less worthy reasons for Christian contributions.

2. What is a most worthy and helpful reason?

3. How does a sense of partnership with God help?

4. What is wrong with spasmodic or occasional contributing?

5. What is the weakness in giving in response to spellbinding appeals?

6. What should we do with the idea of *giving to relieve God's need?*

7. What is lacking in all these methods?

8. What is meant by systematic giving?

9. What is meant by proportional giving?

10. In what way does tithing make an approach to recognition of God's ownership?

11. What mental safeguards should we keep in mind if we adopt the system of tithing?

12. Is tithing the one and only Scriptural method?

13. What is the test of whatever system that we may adopt?

14. What are some of the blessings that come from conscience tithing?

VARIOUS METHODS FOR PRACTICE OF STEWARDSHIP

Individual Laying By in Store

Perhaps the first method to be considered is that which will be practical for the largest number of people. When the Christian has concluded that he is a steward, he should formulate some personal plan by which possessions are to be administered. We might call this Christian budgeting. A Christian who recognizes that even a part of what he possesses is truly God's, to be administered for Him, should determine, according to his best light and Christian development, what part is to be sacredly conserved for strictly Christian work. We are not forgetting that God's plans comprehend the home, the family, the nation, the needy of the community, and all such. None of these is strictly profane or strictly mundane, so is comprehended in Christian stewardship or Christian budgeting.

However, budgeting calls for separation of funds. Those for the enterprises of the church of the living God and Christian charities should be kept separate and ready for use at all times, i. e., "laid by in store," as Paul puts it. Some speak of such as God's bank," on which to draw, or "God's treasury." The amount therein or proportion must be determined according to one's state of growth in Christian stewardship, knowledge, and conscience. This is at least a beginning in the stewardship which should and, if conscientiously followed, will grow as the Christian grows in grace and appreciation of what Christ and the church and membership therein means to him. The amount set aside for this particular work necessarily varies under different circumstances. There are, no doubt, many cases where a widowed mother has to strive inordinately to gather enough in pennies to pay for even poor shelter and a half-ration of needed food for her children. On the other hand, another could set aside a tenth and still have an abundance for all worthy needs and a plenteous sum left over. The amount should be *proportionate* to income or, as the Scriptures put it, "Upon the first day of the week let every one of you lay by him in store, as God hath prospered him, that there be no gatherings when I come" (1 Corinthians 16: 2). A tithe is a good norm to aim for as the beginning of a life of stewardship.

Larger Appropriations From Accumulated Funds

Many persons become Christians after several years have gone by in which they have not recognized God as their partner nor themselves as His. In the meantime, they have conserved and accumulated considerable of earthly assets. They may wish to make up for these lost years and are able to do so.

In such cases there are a number of ways that can be used. Among these are: (1) direct appropriations for the benefit of the local church; (2) appropriations to home and foreign missions; (3)

appropriations to Christian benevolent institutions; (4) appropriations to Christian educational institutions for training ministers, missionaries, and other Christian workers.

Note that these funds are placed by the Christian immediately in the hands of the chosen individuals or institutions ready for immediate use in teaching the untaught, reaching the unreached, and clothing, feeding, and sheltering the needy.

There is a great soul satisfaction in these procedures, for the Christian has a chance to see the resulting work from the funds he has appropriated. Note that we use the term "appropriated" instead of "gave." The Christian who recognizes God's ownership and his own stewardship can *appropriate* from God's wealth but he could not *give*.

Wills and Bequests

When a Christian is preparing to leave this world and depart for the beyond, it is wise and customary to direct disposal of his possesssions by a will, which is legally recognized and safeguarded by the courts. There is a wide field here. While there may be need to provide future protection and even support for wife and children or other dependents, should not the church of Christ and Christian work be included? Many godly souls have thus continued to have a part in the work Christ came to do, after they have finished their days here on earth. While the steward may not be present to see the work accomplished, and while he must trust to the conscience and loyalty of others to administer the funds as he intended, yet here is a happy way for the Christian to say farewell to his possessions and send them on and on to do God's will for him.

Annuities and Perpetual Funds

Provision has been made by many Christian agencies whereby an elderly couple may turn over all or a considerable portion of their possessions to a legally organized missionary, educational, or benevolent agency with the arrangement that so long as either shall live, a fixed annual income shall be paid by the agency; but at the demise of both, the obligation of the agency ends. They may, however, even designate the purpose for which the money is to be used and thus see it work for God and yet bring them their needed support while they live.

Again, funds may be entrusted which may not be spent by the handling agency but are to be invested as a *permanent* fund and the income to be used in perpetuity for some designated worthy cause. One flaw here is that the word "perpetuity" is a big word, and comprehends all future time in a world of continuous changes. There remains the chance that time or disregardful agents may divert the intention of the steward.

Endowments

Where funds are appropriated as a perpetual sustaining fund for some educational purpose or institution, the term "endowment" is usually used.

[69]

The total fund will include money from many donors. Again, this fund must be invested and the proceeds only used as a sustaining fund. Naturally, there are business risks such as are involved in any earthly investment. Monetary panics might wipe the investment out, or trustees might disregard the steward's intent and annul his worthy intent after his death.

Foundations

Because of the tendencies of trustees to re-interpret the intent of those who appropriated the fund, or because once worthy institutions may change and become unworthy, some godly men of wealth have attempted to avoid the possibility of the diverting of the funds to unintended and even unworthy ends, and have devised the "Foundation." Again this is a fund from one or number of individuals to be invested and the income used by carefully chosen trustees only for carefully designated and described purposes. The originator of the fund appoints the first trustees after careful choice, and designates certain requirements or qualifications for succeeding trustees to be appointed by the first ones. Thus it is hoped to avoid the pitfalls that beset the way of permanent funds. To date this seems to be the most satisfactory arrangement for safeguarding the future of large funds whether designated for education and religious enterprises or for benevolent causes and is suggested for your serious consideration.

Various Methods for Practice of Stewardship

Stewardship of Time and Service

The main body of this lesson has been devoted to suggestions as to how money and wealth may play their part in Christian stewardship. We dare not forget that *time* and *talent* are to be as carefully devoted as money. Of uncounted numbers of ways in which this may be done by any Christian, we enumerate a few:

1. *Spreading Christian Good Will and Cheer.* This old world is full of people bowed under burdens and sorrows. We can make it a rule of our Christian stewardship to dispense cheer, kindness, and sympathetic interest. One couple made it the rule of their lives to do some kindly act for some one, worthy or unworthy, each day. A Christian's smile or cheery word may serve like a healing balm for some burdened soul. Think not that this is not a part of a Christian's stewardship.

2. *The Orphan and the Poor.* Aside from orphans' homes, which may be supported by money, there are yet thousands upon thousands of heart-hungry, mother-hungry, and father-hungry children who know not the joy even one day in the year of having a real home life. There are countless homes without children. What an opportunity for Christian stewardship! It was the writer's pleasure to come to know a Christian couple who were ordinary working people but who had taken one or two little children at a time and reared them. When we last saw them, some of the children had grown, but they had just taken in a two-year-old baby girl as

their fourteenth. Again, this is stewardship of one of God's most precious gifts.

3. *Teaching the Gospel to the Untaught.* What a wealth of gospel knowledge is locked up in the heads of thousands of Christians and never shared with the souls of the unsaved! Hiring a minister to do our preaching and teaching is not enough. Every Christian should teach some one else. This is the Bible way and the only way the world will ever be won to Christ. Again, this is stewardship of time and talent. Shall we give account of this stewardship before the great white throne? What an ocean of gospel preaching and teaching has been poured over the heads of thousands of us Christians who have never, in turn, taught another! For one who would learn how to do this service there are a number of plain books of instruction, usually designated as personal evangelism.

QUESTIONS FOR STUDY AND TEACHING

1. What is a first move in adopting a systematic method of contribution?

2. What would be meant by Christian budgeting?

3. Why is it wise in Christian budgeting to separate the funds?

4. How must each determine what proportion is to be set aside for strictly Christian work?

5. What is meant by proportionate giving?

6. What is good norm to adopt as a beginning?

7. Where one has lived out of Christ for many

years and meantime contributed little or nothing, although he has accumulated means, how could the wasted time be made up?

8. What are some of the many causes to which these larger contributions can be well-given?

9. How many Christians through wills continue to have partnership with God?

10. What is meant by annuities and how do they work?

11. What dangers await permanent funds?

12. What is to be said of endowments?

13. What is the advantage of the "Foundation" and how does it work?

14. Name a number of ways in which stewardship of time and service may be practiced by any Christian.

THE STEWARD'S FURTHER RESPONSIBILITY

Responsibility Does Not End With the Allotting of Funds by a Steward

Even the most conscientious and many of the faithful, systematic, and proportionately contributing stewards seem to feel their their whole co-operation with God is fulfilled when the wherewithal has been provided for any particular Christian work or enterprise. The purpose of this lesson is to try to plant and fix the conviction that responsibility for the outcome is as definite as is the responsibility for contributing. The steward's responsibility is not completed until the end sought by the means is accomplished.

Make note of Jesus' parable of the stewards and the pounds or talents. The money is the Lord's; the steward has directed it to advance some particular work of God, perhaps in some particular place. Simply turning the fund over to the hands of another does not complete stewardship responsibility.

As It Applies to the Local Church

The suggestions made in the first paragraph do not apply so much to funds for the support of the local church. There has usually been a bare sufficiency to take care of the apparent and necessary needs in support of the local church program. Certainly there is no intention of suggesting a dictatorial attitude on the part of every contributor. The New Testament provides for the plan of operating the local church under the guidance of the elders as the spiritual overseers of the flock and deacons who are to give conscientious time to the monetary, physical, and charitable work of the church.

The New Testament provides a way for safeguarding and properly handling the joint contributions made by the members for the work of the congregation. The New Testament plan is for the members to choose carefully the best available men who are Scripturally eligible, and set them apart as elders or spiritual overseers of the flock, and deacons for the duties previously stated. If the members do their duty in making these choices, it is then in order to entrust the general handling of the congregation's funds to these men who are subject to the directions or approval of the congregation. This does not limit the Christian freedom of any member, however, to allocate from the Lord's money directly to such special Christian work as he may choose.

The Congregation as a Forwarding Agency

It is right, proper, and convenient to have the congregation or a special committee serve as a forwarding agency for funds to Christian enterprises chosen or designated by the donor or chosen by the congregation. This helps eleminate confusion and is conducive to good order. Also a tested agency may be so used.

[75]

A Need for Safeguards

Where considerable amounts of money are to be expended for enterprises outside of the congregation there arises a need for a safeguard. This is due to a characteristic which has marked men in all nations since the beginning of recorded history. Money in quantity has ever had a tremendous lure for man; not only its accumulation but its control and expenditure. Jesus, in His teaching on covetousness showed that He recognized this weakness, or human ambition.

Even Sacred Money Needs Safeguarding

The head to this paragraph is by no means intended to suggest dishonesty. However, as earnest souls try to re-enforce the spread of the gospel by building up large income-earning, permanent funds, they are forced to remember that this age-old characteristic of mortals still survives and no doubt will so long as time lasts. People are only people.

Let us keep in mind that a steward's responsibility does not end with providing means. The money is God's and must not be diverted to ends that are contrary to the purpose of Christ, the Master.

The occasion for the need of care and safeguarding is that the present-day world is filled with ever-blooming human philosophies, ideas, schemes, and plans promoted by enthusiasts for their particular scheme for the uplift of people and the bringing to each and all the "abundant life." Jesus did not send His apostles out to work to see that there was "a chicken in every pot and two cars in every garage." He did say, "Go ye into all the world, and preach the gospel to every creature" (Mark 16: 15). Paul says, "For I am not ashamed of the gospel of Christ: for it is the power of God unto salvation" (Romans 1: 16). An unconverted panhandler may be dressed up in finest style, but unless his heart is changed, he is still a panhandler. A naked heathen might be taught to wear fine clothes, but unless his heart is changed he is yet a heathen.

Sacred Christian money should not be diverted to meet the calls and schemes of every philosophy of the social uplifters. The larger the pile of conse-crated money, the greater temptation it is for men who are not controlled by the gospel to want to get hold of its direction. These men may not be dis-honest, according to their lights, and may be entire-ly sincere in their aims, but their plans and aims are not the same as those laid down by the Christ. Interests *well outside the fold* seek to get such men on trusteeships and directorates of institutions origi-nally planned and financed to glorify the Christ and promote the preaching of His Word. This applies to so-called Christian educational institutions and to agencies directing the work of world-wide evange-lism, and of any kind of Christian work for the needy, the sick, and the homeless.

Two Future Needs as to Christian Money

There are two needs in regard to funds set aside strictly for God's work. One is that the Christian world be imbued with the knowledge and spirit of Christian stewardship to the point where funds provided for God's work will be ample to carry on that work to the farthermost confines of earth and to all nations, tribes, and tongues. This need has been emphasized by thousands of ministers, teachers, and writers.

It is the second need that we wish to emphasize in this paragraph because it has not been generally emphasized. That need is that we be spiritually equipped in wisdom, loyalty, and devotion to direct the expenditure of this money to the ends to which it is consecrated. To illustrate: Suppose that this year every member of your own congregation should begin to set aside regularly and systematically an average of one-tenth of his income. What in your judgment would be the amount turned in as compared with the present income? Figure it out.

Again: Suppose every follower of Christ in the United States should this year do the same. According to figures from the United States Department of Commerce for 1949, the total expenditures for the year, by us all, amounted to $178,800,000,-000. Approximately one-half of our population is connected with some church—Catholic or Protestant. This allegedly Christian half, including the rich and the poor, spent one-half of this vast amount, or $89,400,000,000. If every one in the Christian group turned in a tithe, the total amount would be $8,940,000,000. That is for one year, then a like amount each year. The purpose of this paragraph is to raise the question, are we spiritually equipped in conviction, loyalty, and devotion to Christ and His Word to direct this mighty flood of funds as Christ would have it? Are we now equipped spiritually, and with present methods, to avoid allowing this flood of gold to sound the death knell of spirituality, and of the church for which Christ died?

To read the history of the church one is frightened and dismayed. During one period of history in England, the church actually owned one-half of all English assets. Luxury among prelates prevailed, sin among the people ran riot, and corruption prostituted and displaced the proclamation of the Word of God.

As we teach, work, hope, pray for the opening of Christian hearts to Christian stewardship of money, is it not quite as important at this stage that we teach the Christian his full responsibility, the need for wisdom, and consecration in handling God's money for Him? We raise the question because we feel that it is necessary in any study of Christian stewardship. The answer to this question must be discovered by each Christian.

Warning

Frequently, when securing a prescription of perfectly good medicine at the drug store for some ailment, we find pasted on the bottle the word "Warning." In this case we append the warning. Nothing presented in this study is intended as a criticism, a suspicion of or accusation of any individuals or agencies. The teaching is for us all as stewards. Certainly we would not want to give any one reason to decrease God's special portion or to withhold. There is not and probably never will be too much money for God's work. The weakness is not in the money but in us. This is true if we come to look upon money as a sure means to save the world or if we become careless in the handling or directing of the money that is God's.

We might make the point clear by a homely illustration. A little boy had a large, tasty birthday cake. He was helped a third time and then turned it down. His father said, "What's the matter Johnnie, did I give you too much birthday cake?" "No," said Johnnie, "there ain't no such thing as too much cake. The trouble is there just ain't enough boy."

What is needed is more loyal consecration, not less, in providing and handling the wherewithal to carry on the work of Christ's kingdom.

QUESTIONS FOR STUDY AND TEACHING

1. Does a Christian steward's responsibility end with the mere furnishing of means?

2. How far and to what end does this responsibility extend?

3. What is the New Testament plan for safeguarding funds of a local church?

4. How may the officers of a congregation serve as a forwarding agency for the individual?

5. Why does the need arise for special safeguards for larger and permanent funds?

6. What gives rise in this day to the need for safeguards?

7. Is the political conception of "the abundant life" the same as the Christian conception?

8. What does the non-Christian, poor or rich, need most?

9. What are the two outstanding needs as to Christian stewardship?

10. If the ideal of Christian stewardship should be adopted and prevail are we spiritually equipped to handle the outpouring?

11. How could an outpouring of wealth affect the church?

12. Do the needed safeguards justify us in withholding or simply show the need for continued responsibility on the part of the donor?

13. What then is the chief need as to direction and stewardship of the wherewithal to carry on the work of Christ?

THE DEVELOPMENT OF A STEWARDSHIP CONSCIENCE AND PRACTICE

Steps in the Development of Christian Stewardship

Seed must be planted if a crop is to be reaped. Jesus gave us an illustration that is pertinent here. "And he said, So is the kingdom of God, as if a man should cast seed into the ground; and should sleep, and rise night and day, and the seed should spring and grow up, he knoweth not how. For the earth bringeth forth fruit of herself; first the blade, then the ear, after that the full corn in the ear" (Mark 4: 26-28). Flowers do not just burst forth. First the seed helped by sunshine and soil, then the plant, then the bud, and finally the full bloom.

The Christian graces follow the same law of growth. In some, the growth is more rapid than in others. Nature makes allowances for effects of soil, moisture, and sun. Some Christian lives develop more rapidly than others. Soil and sunshine, spiritually speaking, having their influence.

"The seed is the word of God" (Luke 8: 11). Consistently we revert to something said in a preceding lesson. The whole Christian development scheme comprehends a *planting* and a *growth*. Every Christian virtue springs from the implanted seed of the Word. Some seeds merely sprout. Some sprout and grow a bit and are choked out. All these truths obtain in the process of the conviction, concep-

[82]

tion, development, and growth of the grace of Christian stewardship. It can hardly be forced, but if planted and nourished the seed of the Word of God will grow.

The Seed

As it has been stated, the Word of God is the seed. The human heart is the soil. The first step, as was suggested, is the planting of the seed. This means a reading and rereading of the New Testament Scriptures or the whole Bible, for that matter. Bible reading should have a directing purpose. Too much Bible reading is purposeless except as a holy exercise. Frequently, however, one stumbles onto readings that lead to other fixed purposes. For example, one might read to find out just what to do to *become* a Christian; another might read to know just what a New Testament church is like.

In the matter of stewardship one must read to discover what the Scripture has to say that has a bearing on Christian stewardship of time, talent, and money. This purposeful reading is an absolute requisite if the seed of Christian stewardship is planted and nurtured.

Along with personal reading, listening regularly to the preaching and teaching of the *Word* is an essential. It is true one might listen to much preaching that throws little light on this particular subject, but all good preaching helps create the attitude of further light in all the features of Christian life and practice.

Prayer and Stewardship

Real prayer is a personal communion with God. We come nearer in prayer to standing face to face with God, somewhat as we shall on the judgment day, than at any other time in the day or the week. In prayer we ask for many things. It is certainly legitimate to ask for God's guidance in determining our position and program as to our stewardship with Him. Can we sincerely say, "Thy kingdom come, thy will be done on earth as it is in heaven," without a twinge of conscience that would make us say, "What am I doing to help God's kingdom to come and His will to be done in all the earth?"

Making a Start

Before any one can arrive anywhere, he has to make a start. The start may be a long way from the finish, but the only way to get anywhere is to start. Thinking about it, dallying with it, planning to some day become a Christian steward of God's substance does not get far. The way to start is simply to start. The beginning may seem small or even insignificant or unimportant, but it is of supreme importance. Therefore, in immediate conjunction with reading the Scripture and with sincere prayer on the subject, we should at once *adopt a personal program* of life in which we regularly, systematically, and conscientiously and in some definitely decided proportion, start sharing with God our time, talent, and means. Our start may appear inadequate to the more developed and mature Christians, but if it is made conscientiously, and based on our knowledge of God's Word, this grace will most certainly develop as does any other Christian grace.

Effect on Our Hearts

Let us recall that God's one interest in man is his salvation from sin and development of a Christ-like life and character. We must recognize that *we* are God's, that the *earth* is God's, that all good and perfect gifts such as talent, time, and portions of the earth's wealth, come down from the Father and that we are God's partners as stewards of what He has put in our hands. Thus, true stewardship has a most tremendous drawing power to lead us closer to Him in all that we do and all that we have. Thus is God's purpose in us and for us achieved. It becomes evermore less alluring to do what is wrong in His sight and evermore a delight of delights to do what is right in His sight. Thus are our hearts tempered, molded, and formed in godliness and in soul-satisfying living. The Christian life comes to mean much more than merely being *called* a Christian and belonging to the group of Christians, the church. Real Christian stewardship is a soul-building exercise, and fits precisely into God's main aim for His chlidren.

Results Spiritually in the Church

As an ever larger proportion of the members of the church of Christ are drawn closer in heart and consecration to God and Christ, so is the whole church made more and more into the kind of church that can truly be called a church of Christ or *Christian* church. Less selfishness and self-glorification, and more and more real consecration will mark it. More real zeal for the winning of the unsaved will be found and the number of Christians prepared and preparing to teach and who do teach others the way of life, will be multiplied. Worship will spring from the heart. Formality will yield to the simple and loyal practices of the New Testament church. The church will become not a mere *organization* but an active *organism,* throbbing with zeal and power.

The Final Step

The final step is the same as the first, i. e., more reading of the Word and prayer. The Christians on Pentecost not only heard the Word, obeyed the instruction of the Holy Spirit in accepting Christ and obeying the gospel, but "they *continued* stedfastly in the apostles' doctrine and fellowship, and in breaking of bread, and in prayers."

So, for a life of Christian stewardship we start wherever the Word finds us. The start is *but the start.* Too often we would count the act of becoming a Christian as final and complete. Human tendency is to do something immediately and count the whole transaction completed. In one sense it is; we are *buried* to the old life, but quite as certainly are we raised to *walk* in newness of life all the rest of our days.

[86]

QUESTIONS FOR STUDY AND TEACHING

1. What is nature's fixed law of production of all things?

2. Do the Christian graces follow the same pattern?

3. As to Christian life and growth, what is the seed?

4. What is the soil in which the seed is to be planted?

5. To develop the grace of Christian stewardship how must we search the Scriptures?

6. How is prayer conducive to Christian stewardship?

7. What is the way to start building the practice of stewardship?

8. Can we expect growth in Christian stewardship from what appears to be even a small beginning?

9. What basic truth must ever be kept in mind?

10. What effect will faithful practice have on our hearts?

11. What results would surely appear in the church as a whole as a larger proportion of the membership is drawn closer in heart to God?

ABILITY OF CHRIST'S CHURCH TO MEET THE CHALLENGE

Open Doors

Some have said that when the Christians of the world recognize the principle of stewardship of wealth the church will be financially able to open doors for the gospel in all lands and to all tribes and tongues. As a matter of fact, doors are already open in abundance. What we need to do is to enter in with the gospel, which is the "power of God unto salvation." Read the letters of any foreign missionary in any land, however backward that land may be and each letter reveals a picture of open doors.

With American itself only half Christian, even nominally, read the letters of ministers who are imbued with the thought and Scriptural teaching that men out of Christ are lost and without hope. Near to or in the grasp of each is a field he points to as an open door for the simple New Testament gospel of Christ.

Look about you in your own town or city. Half the people in the average community are indifferent to the call of Christ and God. Indeed, as Christ said, "The harvest truly is great, but the labourers are few: pray ye therefore the Lord of the harvest, that he would send forth labourers into his harvest" (Luke 10: 2).

Every Christian Can Share

Truly not every one can go, but again truly every one can *go* or *send*. If I furnish or help to furnish the means to send an earnest young couple to preach the Word of truth and hope to the people of Tibet, I am therefore preaching to these people more effectively than I might be able to do personally.

Again Jesus said, "Say not ye, There are yet four months, and then cometh harvest? behold, I say unto you, Lift up your eyes, and look on the fields; for they are white already to harvest" (John 4: 35). This Scripture in effect says, "Now."

A general awakening to stewardship would enable truly consecrated heralds of the gospel, who are ready and willing to go into every field from the frozen poles of the North to the sunwarmed lands of the equator, or from the mountains of Madagascar or Tibet to the plains of China and Siberia. The doors *are* open.

Temporarily, some doors are closed by political upheavals, but these upheavals are not new and will end. *Aside from this* there are innumerable open doors *now*, at home and abroad. We can each be active co-operators with God and enter in.

Hungry Mouths To Be Fed

"Lift up your eyes, and look on the fields." If every adherent to the cause of Christ were conscientiously serving as a steward for God, how many hungry children could be fed! Let us remember that there are uncounted thousands of children in God's world, who have never once known what it means to have one full and satisfying wholesome meal. This is not imagination, but a tragic fact. Our own lives are short. Shall we hang onto our shekels, dollars, or pounds until death releases our grip and we go serenely on to the end, untouched by want, hunger, and physical starvation? Jesus said, "I was an hungred, and ye gave me meat: I was thirsty, and ye gave me drink: I was a stranger, and ye took me in: naked, and ye clothed me: I was sick, and ye visited me: I was in prison, and ye came unto me. Then shall the righteous answer him, saying, Lord, when saw we thee an hungered, and fed thee? or thirsty, and gave thee drink? when saw we thee a stranger, and took thee in? or naked, and clothed thee? or when saw we thee sick, or in prison, and came unto thee? And the King shall answer and say unto them, Verily I say unto you, Inasmuch as ye have done it unto one of the least of these my brethren, ye have done it unto me" (Matthew 25: 35-40).

Here in this short bit of Scripture is a whole lesson on Christian stewardship. If I provide from God's money or means in my hands, the wherewithal to make possible such acts, I certainly am as much a steward as the one who hands out the bread. General stewardship on the part of individual Christians would expand the power for such Christian practice beyond our present ability to imagine.

The Purpose of This Lesson

The purpose of this lesson is to cause us each to *stop, look,* and *listen* to the multiplied opportunities for the practice of Christlike Christianity. In this lesson we take a look at "what could be if . . ."

It is true that some of the fields on which Christ told us to look are so far away that we can only dimly visualize them. A starving child in Asia does not impress us as would one next door, but Christ's instruction included the whole world (Matthew 28:19). We might feel that this is not *preaching* the Word, but it is *practicing* the Word and opening hearts to hear the preached Word. Best of all it is opening our own hearts, and this is God's desire and purpose in making stewards of every Christian. Truly the growth of vision in stewardship, of time, talent, and means is a God-given privilege and never was intended to be a burdensome obligation upon any one.

Shall Some Starve for the Bread of Life?

We who live in America live in the most blessed land on earth. Physically, we are blessed beyond all other peoples, in goods, conveniences, cash, luxuries, and opportunities for relaxation and pleasure. In addition, we are in a free land where no one is going to be imprisoned or penalized for reading or teaching the Word of God. This is not the case in many lands. Let us all give thanks that it is so in the United States of America.

What use do we make of this freedom? Truly

we would all rise up in loud protest if these rights were threatened, but what use are we making of them?

A Christian knows what the Word says to do to be saved. It is so simple any one could teach another. Yet in our own America we are told that there are thirty-seven million children and youth growing up as untaught in the Word of God as though they lived in the African jungle. Does the Scriptural ideal and principle of stewardship involve no responsibility on the part of each of us or these coming Americans? Shall we leave them to the mercies of wild-eyed political faddists and fanatics who hate the very idea of God and push an active campaign to eliminate and suppress the teaching of the Word of God? Very probably every Christian on the way to church last Sunday passed a goodly number of these untaught children.

Suppose all Christians should catch a fresh view of their stewardship and each determine to do something about it besides talk and lament over the godless trend. What would be the result of such a concerted move?

Three Co-equal Phases of Christian Stewardship

We must constantly keep in mind that there are not *one* but *three* phases of Christain stewardship. They are stewardship of *time*, stewardship of *talent* or *knowledge*, and stewardship of *means*. We have just faced some of the possibilities of conquest and victory for Christ that can be achieved by the administration or consecration of a bit of time and talent. This must not obscure and does not need to lessen our stewardship of means.

If every Christian should adopt a systematic, proportionate, and regular system of contribution, would so many houses of God be unpainted? Sagging doors hanging on rusty hinges and dilapidation advertise what looks to the unsaved like the weakness of Christ's cause.

Recall Christ's teaching about going out into the highways and byways (see Matthew 22: 9). If every member of even a relatively small congregation were a systematic steward of his income, would even the small congregation lack the means to provide a bus to travel the highways and bring in the unchurched grown folk, as well as the children, for Bible instruction? If every Christian, as a steward, should hold a private dedication service for his own car and dedicate a part of the use of it to the service of God, how many millions of miles could be traveled in the name of Christ? If every Christian man, woman, or young person, having a telephone should dedicate a reasonable share of the use of it to God's service and call and invite people to ride to the preaching service next Sunday, how many churches would have empty seats, or how many unsaved could be brought out of the highways to "the highway" that leads to eternal life?

The students in this study can no doubt add many ideas to these definite suggestions of stewardship of time, property, and service.

[93]

Studies in Christian Stewardship

Are We Equipped to Practice Christian Stewardship?

As a means to help us to see clearly, the possibility of solving any financial problem of the works of God, Christ, and the church, we append some government official figures of expenditures in the United States of America for 1949:

1. Goods and services .... 179 Billions
2. Alcoholic beverages .... 8¾ Billions
3. Gambling .... 21½ Billions
4. Tobacco .... 4⅓ Billions
5. Soft drinks .... 1 Billion
6. Motion pictures .... 1½ Billions
7. Beauty Parlor and Barber .... ½ Billion
8. Recreation .... 4 Billions
9. Education .... 6½ Billions
10. Church Contributions .... 1½ Billions

With the exception of item 10, which we must presume was contributed wholly by Christians, we can total all the other items and divide by two, to get the amount spent for these items by the one-half our population that is allegedly Christian. These figures given above total forty-eight billions. One-half of this is twenty-four billions. Hence the followers of Christ spent last year for the items here listed twenty-four billions and for church contributions one and one-half billions. We did not include most of the items listed in the government figures such as food, clothing, housing, etc. We have here listed only those items that are luxuries or wholly unnecessary, in order to set them over against what is contributed to the churches for all work at home and abroad and for education.

These figures are given merely to cause us each to ask the question, could we increase materially the proportion allotted to God's work.

QUESTIONS FOR STUDY AND TEACHING

1. Where can we find open doors for the practice of Christian stewardship of means, time, and talent? . Illustrate.

2. What did Christ say as to the harvest?

3. How could every Christian share even in work that is remote?

4. What would be the result of a general awakening of Christians to Christian stewardship?

5. What did Jesus say about service to even the least?

6. How does His saying apply to Christian stewardship?

7. How far should our Christian vision extend?

8. What special opportunities and obligations does America lend us?

9. Are we making use of the freedoms we have?

10. If stewardship of means were practiced, what are some of the things that could be done by even a small congregation?

11. How could we dedicate to God a share in some of our modern conveniences?

12. Compare Christian expenditures for luxuries and for Christian work.

AN EVENING WITH GOD'S WORD

The study closes with a lesson devoted wholly to *Scripture reading*. The Scriptures listed are *but some* of those having a direct or indirect bearing on stewardship. Although we live today under the New Testament and the laws of the Old Testament are displaced by the gospel, yet we include passages from the Old Testament that are *statements of eternal facts or truths* which are not ever displaced. In most instances these facts are stated over and over again in the New Testament.

The intention in this lesson is that the study should be opened with *earnest prayer* and then devoted to the *reading in full* of every passage cited. This can be done easily in the hour. Use your Bibles for the reading.

No arguments or teachings the author of these lessons could submit are comparable to the Word of God. If that does not reach our hearts and lead us to Christian convictions, the humble human author of this text could not hope or expect to do so.

God's Ownership of the World and All Therein

1. *Old Testament Statement of Facts*:

"God created the heaven and the earth" (Genesis 1: 1, 6).

"So God created man in his own image" (Genesis 1: 27).

[96]

"The earth is the Lord's, and the fulness thereof; the world, and they that dwell therein" (Psalm 24: 1).

"Let them [man] have dominion over the fish of the sea, and over the fowl of the air, and over the cattle, and over all the earth, and over every creeping thing that creepeth upon the earth" (Genesis 1: 26). (Note: God conferred dominion, not ownership.)

2. *New Testament Confirmations*:

"All things were created by him, and for him" (Colossians 1: 16).

"Ye are bought with a price" (1 Corinthians 7: 23).

"Ye are Christ's; and Christ is God's" (1 Corinthians 3: 23).

"Every good and every perfect gift is from above, and cometh down from the Father of lights" (James 1: 17).

What Comprises Life

"A man's life consisteth not in the abundance of the things which he possesseth" (Luke 12: 15).

"For what is a man profited, if he shall gain the whole world, and lose his own soul? or what shall a man give in exchange for his soul?" (Matthew 16: 26).

"This night thy soul shall be required of thee: then whose shall those things be, which thou hast provided?" (Luke 12: 20).

Read the entire parable in Luke 12: 16-23.

We Shall All Render an Accounting

"For we shall all stand before the judgment seat of Christ" (Romans 14: 10).

"So then every one of us shall give account of himself to God" (Romans 14: 12).

"Inasmuch as ye have done it unto one of the least of these my brethren, ye have done it unto me" (Matthew 25: 40).

Read the entire passage of Matthew 25: 34-40.

Why God Wants Us to Share as Partners in His Work

"For where your treasure is, there will your heart be also" (Matthew 6: 21).

"Not because I desire a gift: but I desire fruit that may abound to your account" (Philippians 4: 17).

"Whatsoever a man soweth, that shall he also reap" (Galatians 6: 7).

"He that soweth to his flesh shall of the flesh reap corruption; but he that soweth to the Spirit shall of the Spirit reap life everlasting" (Galatians 6: 8).

"He which soweth sparingly shall reap also sparingly; and he which soweth bountifully shall reap also bountifully" (2 Corinthians 9: 6).

A Regular and Proportionate Amount Set Aside

"Upon the first day of the week let every one of you lay by him in store, as God hath prospered him, that there be no gatherings when I come" (1 Corinthians 16: 2).

"As every man hath received a gift, even so minister the same one to another, as good stewards of the manifold grace of God" (1 Peter 4: 10).

"It is required in stewards, that a man be found faithful" (1 Corinthians 4: 2).

God Recognizes Human Needs and Obligations

"Provide things honest in the sight of all men" (Romans 12: 17).

"Providing for honest things, not only in the sight of the Lord, but also in the sight of men" (2 Corinthians 8: 21).

"But if any provide not for his own, and specially for those of his own house, he hath denied the faith, and is worse than an infidel" (1 Timothy 5: 8).

"Render therefore unto Caesar the things which are Caesar's; and unto God the things that are God's" (Matthew 22: 21).

Christ's Model Illustration of Stewardship

Jesus taught and illustrated with parables which any one could understand and remember. While space does not permit incorporating here the entire story of the good Samaritan (Luke 10: 30-37), we cite it to be read. Treasure in mind that the good Samaritan gave service and money to aid one who was a Jew. The Jews despised all Samaritans, but the Samaritan did what the passing priest and Levite should have done. Read the entire passage thoughtfully.

Stewardship Has Many Features

1. *Gratitude to God is one.* Read the Golden Text of the Bible. "For God so loved the world, that he gave his only begotten Son, that whosoever believeth in him should not perish, but have everlasting life" (John 3: 16). Gratitude would lead to faithful stewardship.

2. "The wages of sin is death; but the gift of God is eternal life through Jesus Christ our Lord" (Romans 6: 23). Can we accept such an unimaginable gift without wanting to do something about it?

3. "The Spirit itself beareth witness with our spirit, that we are the children of God: and if children, then heirs; heirs of God, and joint-heirs with Christ" (Romans 8: 16, 17)—*stewards, partners, children, heirs.*

Shall we hear these words of the Master, "Well done, good and faithful servant; thou hast been faithful over a few things, I will make thee ruler over many things: enter thou into the joy of thy Lord"? (Matthew 25: 23).

QUESTIONS FOR STUDY AND TEACHING

1. What is the main purpose of Lesson Thirteen?

2. Quote some basic facts and truths from the Old Testament showing God's ownership.

3. Did God confer ownership or dominion?

4. Quote some New Testament passages restating and confirming these basic truths.

5. What did Jesus say as to the real issues of life?

[100]

6. What does the New Testament say about our final accounting?

7. How does the Lord count even a small service done for even the least?

8. Why does God want us to share in His work in the world?

9. How shall we determine how much to share?

10. How does the New Testament provide for our earthly obligations?

11. What lessons can we all learn from the parable of the good Samaritan?

12. What should be at the basis of our stewardship?

13. Quote some Scriptures showing how gratitude is due to the Lord.

APPENDIX

We deem it well to add, as an appendix, a bit of explanation which did not seem to fit under any of the lesson heads.

1. Many problems will arise in building a life and instigating the practice of Christian stewardship. These problems are different in almost every case. For that reason we have made no attempt to include any stock rules for the solving of these problems for each person. One kind of problem faces the farmer, another the storekeeper, and so on through the entire list. These problems can be solved only by each individual in the light of a

real Christian conscience and the Word of God.

2. An example: A peculiar problem as to proportions, allotments, etc., arises since much that we Christians once counted as a part of our Christian allowance for the needy, the sick, the jobless, and the untaught, has been taken over by the national and state governments. We are taxed to pay for this charitable service once rendered by appropriations of stewardship funds. The service is rendered in the name of the government instead of in the name of Christ. Hence this problem: Should we figure our share in this service as a part of our stewardship account? No one can solve this problem for another.

3. Our study has therefore proceeded with the task of a restudy of the whole subject from the standpoint of the teachings of Christ and the apostles. If our vision can be lifted up above the practices that have come down to us, based on habit instead of Scriptural knowledge, then we shall have accomplished much indeed. If we can all be drawn closer to God and to our Saviour and to the Word of God, we shall have found the one permanent approach to our mundane relationship and duty to our Father in heaven. If our hearts can be rebathed in the sunlight of God's love as revealed in the Word, we shall in time find the answers. When we find and adopt these answers, the cause of Christ will not languish. It will have a new birth of victories for Him and a new triumphant joy for those who are His.